O9-BRZ-363

OPEN YOUR HEARTS

Prayer Exercises for Engaged and Newly Married Couples

Carol Luebering

ST.
ANTHONY
MESSENGER
PRESS

CINCINNATI, OHIO

Nihil Obstat: Rev. Robert J. Buschmiller
Rev. Lawrence Landini, O.F.M.

Imprimi Potest: Rev. John Bok, O.F.M.
Provincial

Imprimatur: +James H. Garland, V.G.
Archdiocese of Cincinnati
September 5, 1991

The *nihil obstat* and *imprimatur* are a declaration that a book is considered to be free from doctrinal or moral error. It is not implied that those who have granted the *nihil obstat* and *imprimatur* agree with the contents, opinions or statements expressed.

Scripture citations are taken from *The New Revised Standard Version Bible,* copyright ©1989 by the Division of Christian Education of the National Council of the Churches of Christ in the USA and are used by permission. All rights reserved.

"The Canticle of Brother Sun" is taken from *St. Francis of Assisi: Writings and Early Biographies English Omnibus of the Sources for the Life of St. Francis* published by Franciscan Herald Press, Chicago, Illinois, with translations by Raphael Brown, Benen Fahy, Placid Hermann, Paul Oligny, Nesta de Robeck and Leo Sherley-Price.

Excerpts from the English translation of *Rite of Marriage* © 1969, International Committee on English in the Liturgy, Inc. (ICEL); excerpts from the English translation of *The Roman Missal* © 1973, ICEL. All rights reserved.

Cover and book design by Julie Lonneman

ISBN 0-86716-162-0

©1991, Carol Luebering
All rights reserved.

Published by St. Anthony Messenger Press
Printed in the U.S.A.

Contents

Introduction

Praying Together

Married lovers pray together many times and in many ways. And so will you—all through the years of your life together.

Your hearts will acknowledge the nearness of the God who *is* love when you make love to one another. You will kneel side by side in church on Sundays; you will clasp hands in silent awe before the wonders of nature, before the miracle of a newborn child. When worry or sorrow invades your life, you will storm heaven for comfort. And you will, of course, pray for each other in good times and bad.

But praying together—really *together*—is more than just praying side by side. Praying together means entering into each other's prayer, making prayer a three-way conversation with the God who gave you to one another. And it is an enriching experience of intimacy, an opening of the deepest recesses of your hearts to one another in the presence of Love itself.

Like any other movement toward intimacy, praying together requires experimentation and practice. You may feel awkward or foolish or ill at ease in the beginning. This book, I hope, will ease you into shared prayer.

Its structure is very simple. It borrows a pattern from a devotion popular a few decades ago: the novena. The word means "nine"; to "make a novena" means to repeat a certain prayer nine times—usually over a period of nine weeks.

The concept has roots deep in Christian history. The first novena is described in the opening chapter of the Acts of the Apostles. The followers of Jesus returned to Jerusalem after he ascended from their sight. They gathered in the upper room where they had celebrated the Last Supper with him and prayed together for nine days until the promised Spirit exploded into their lives.

The novena in these pages explores nine different kinds of prayer. All are drawn from the rich tradition of Christian prayer. Most of them have something of a familiar feel, for you have encountered them at liturgy and in other prayer experiences. And all of them draw from the experience of lovers entering marriage.

Set aside a little time each day to pray your way through this book for nine days. You don't need to carve much out of your busy schedule; half an hour will probably serve. And you need little else: something to eat and drink together on Day Four, an optional bottle of holy water for Day Five and a Bible for Day Six.

Let these days make a small oasis of quiet before your wedding or integrate them into your honeymoon discovery of each other. But remember that they are intended just as a beginning, a set of exercises to practice again over a lifetime of praying together.

You may discover one kind of prayer that is most comfortable to both of you and settle into it as your pattern for praying together. But a novena can be repeated. This little journey through prayer will be different each time you make it together because you—your experience, your hopes and dreams, your love and knowledge of God and of each other—will change and grow. The novena can change and grow, too. At the end of this book you'll find some suggestions for reshaping it.

You are sacrament, so you've been told, a living sign of God's presence among us. In your love the rest of us catch a reflection of a God passionately in love with the human race. You are sacrament to each other as well. In your life together, in the joy of making love and the work of reaching across differences to become ever more one, you too will catch glimpses of God. May your shared conversations with the divine Lover enrich your life together.

Day One

Being Still

Remember how simple life was before you started planning a wedding? No endless lists tucked into your pocket, no host of details to worry about, no frantic pace and endless fatigue. You had time to waste together, time to be alone together, time just to *be* together in silence.

Some of the most precious moments lovers spend together pass in silence: walking with an arm around a waist, sitting by a fire head to shoulder, dancing cheek to cheek, lying in each other's arms after making love. No words are necessary. You just soak up each other's presence with all your senses. And if one of you breaks the silence, the other may well whisper, "Sshh!"

The divine lover also whispers, "Sshh":

"Be still, and know that I am God!"
(Psalm 46:10)

Being still before God, being caught up in God's presence, is the prayer called *contemplation*. Called the highest form of prayer by spiritual writers, contemplation is the prayer of the great mystics. It sent St. Catherine of Siena into ecstasies and moved St. John of the Cross to poetry.

But contemplation is not just for great saints. It was most simply defined by an old man who explained why he liked just to sit in an empty church: "I look at him and he looks at me." In our time it has become popular as "centering prayer" or in meditation techniques.

Theologians make fine distinctions among different kinds of contemplation, but for our purposes it is simply quieting oneself in God's presence. A good way to begin any kind of prayer, it requires an attentive silence that listens for the barest whisper of God's movement. It is first a time of waiting, of searching, of becoming aware of God's nearness.

Spiritual writer James Carroll once compared becoming aware of God's presence to a child's hidden picture puzzle where a face is concealed in the outline of a cloud or in the branches of a tree. At first it is invisible, but once its outline is traced, the face jumps out every time the child looks at the picture again.

People discover God's presence in just the same way. Sometimes they see God outside themselves: In a cathedral of giant redwoods or a spring-kissed garden divine fingerprints suddenly appear, and nature-lovers seek the quiet spot at the seaside or in the woods to recreate the experience.

Others experience an interior encounter. Centering prayer turns one's attention deep within where God dwells in each of us. Or the realization of sinfulness in our hearts may hail God's nearness. An 18th-century unbeliever found himself crying out in prayer during a storm at sea. Years later, slave trader turned minister John Newton lent words later set to music for future generations to express the same knowledge: "Amazing grace...that saved a wretch like me."

Finding love shouts of God's presence—God's finger on one's shoulder, someone once called it. Scripture affirms that insight: "God is love, and those who abide in love abide in God, and God abides in them" (1 John 4:16b).

Contemplation—being attentive to God's presence—is surely, then, a natural prayer for lovers to share. This first prayer of your novena is an invitation to look for hints of God's presence both within you and between you, in the love which binds you. All this exercise asks of you is to sit together in silent attentiveness, aware of the love in which you abide and the Love who abides in you.

This prayer cannot be hurried. It takes time to quiet your mind and relax your body. It takes time to settle into silence and become aware of God's presence there.

Choose a comfortable spot. Sit close together with your bodies just touching each other. Hold hands, if you like, close your eyes and relax physically and mentally. Listen to the silence until you become accustomed to all the little background sounds that invade it. Listen to your own breathing and the breathing of the one you love.

Focus on the love in your own heart, on the love in your lover's heart. Warm yourselves with the one love you share. Feel its presence all around you. Know that God moves in it and through it. Rest together in the Source of all love.

Naming the Mystery

"Let me call you sweetheart" begs a song popular at the turn of the century. A much older love song, the biblical Song of Solomon, addresses the lover as "my love," "my fair one" and "my dove." For reasons known only to themselves, one modern couple call each other "Bird" and "Bear." Given names, it seems, are inadequate for lovers. They bestow on each other names which express, at least to them, the relationship between them.

Believers have always done the same. Scripture scholars untangle the threads of authorship in the oldest books of the Bible partly by noting what names the writers use for God: Yahweh or El. When Moses met God in the burning bush, he asked what he should call the flame which, like love, burned without destroying (see Exodus 3:1-15).

"What's in a name?" Juliet asked Romeo. "A rose by any other name would smell as sweet." Yet in Leonard Bernstein's musical version of Shakespeare's tale, *West Side Story*, the hero sings a virtual hymn to the name *Maria*—for a name with a personal history attached is much more than just a handy label. The names lovers give each other, the names by which believers call on God reflect their discovery of mystery, the unfolding of wonder, an image of the one named.

Today's prayer is an exploration of your images of God as revealed in the names you use in prayer. It asks you to compose a *litany*, calling on God by all the names that reflect your understanding and your relationship with God.

A litany is usually a series of short invocations with a response. The litany of the saints names many *people*: "St. Joseph, pray for us. St. Martha, pray for us." The Litany of Loretto addresses Mary by many *titles*: "Mother of Christ," "Mystical Rose," "Queen of heaven." The Litany of the Holy Name rolls out the titles of Jesus: "Jesus, Son of the living God, Good Shepherd, Prince of Peace, have mercy on us."

Most familiar are the two short litanies of the Mass. They too address Jesus. "You came to call sinners; Lord, have mercy," we pray as the liturgy begins, and you have heard that formula varied many times. Just before Communion comes the Lamb of God, which in some parishes is prolonged in song with more phrases which describe what Jesus does: "Lamb of God, you heal the brokenhearted."

Your litany can borrow from all of these, addressing more than one divine person, using different titles and/or telling what God does for you. Before you begin, consider these questions individually:

1) To whom do you pray? We profess faith in one God, but also in three Persons: Father, Son and Spirit. Which Person or Persons do you usually call on?

2) What image does that Person have for you? Do you see the God Jesus called Father as creator, judge, tender daddy, lover, mother, warrior? Is Jesus healer, teacher, suffering servant, friend? Is the Spirit powerful, quiet, loving, creative?

3) What has the God to whom you pray done for you and your world? What do you hope God will do?

Sit together as you did on the first day. Spend a few minutes in silence, becoming aware of God's presence, and then address the God you know in your own words. You can shape a petition as part of your prayer, if you wish ("Jesus, gentle friend, walk with us"). Or you might want to say why you give this name to God ("Creator God, I sense your power whenever I look at the stars"). Take your time and let your prayer arise as it will.

When you have finished naming God, talk about the images your prayer expressed. Were either of you surprised by the other's images of God? How different were your prayers? How alike? Talk about how you came to see God as you do.

Day Three

Praising God

"Why do you love me?" Eve perhaps first asked that question. Adam's attempt to answer may have been his expression of delight in one who "at last is bone of my bones/and flesh of my flesh" (Genesis 2:23a). In any case, since a time lost in the dust of history until today, lovers ask why and try to offer answers: "Because of the way your nose crinkles when you laugh." "For your sense of humor." "Because you are beautiful" (or wise or good). "Just because you are you."

There is no real rationale to love. It is pure mystery, a magical gift, and it defies explanation. Both the question and the answers acknowledge that truth. They do not seize the reasons. They only frame wonder, and they frame it with praise of the beloved's charms.

And not only praise of the beloved: the world looks different to lovers' eyes. Stars are brighter, sunsets are rosier, fall more breathtaking and spring more heartbreaking. Places once too familiar to be noticed are landmarks of love: the theater where you first saw a movie together, the park where you walked and first spoke of love, the streets that lead to a lover's home. Love songs echo the heart's wonder at a world suddenly clothed with beauty because it is

13

wondrously transformed by love.

Wonder begets praise. Praise attempts to capture wonder in words, to speak the reasons which elude rational grasp. It is as much the language of believers as of lovers, for believers too have been surprised by Love. "All creation gives you praise," says the most familiar Eucharistic Prayer (III).

On the first two days of this novena, you turned your attention to God's presence in and through your love; you named who God is for you. Today's prayer invites you to turn your attention to what God *does* and to create your own song or canticle of praise in response.

Since the dawn of Judeo-Christian belief, believers have sung such songs. Probably the most familiar canticle is Mary's Magnificat:

> My soul magnifies the Lord,
>   and my spirit rejoices in God my savior,
> for he has looked with favor on the lowliness
>   of his servant.
>   Surely, from now on all generations will
>   call me blessed;
> for the Mighty One has done great things for
>   me,
>   and holy is his name. (Luke 1:47-49)

Mary's canticle, the one she sang when she went to share the wonder of incipient motherhood with her cousin Elizabeth, echoes the faith of her people. From childhood she learned of a God who had rescued Israel from oppression in Egypt and showed compassion for the poor. She recalls the promises made to her ancestors as she rejoices at the promise fulfilled in her own flesh.

St. Francis of Assisi drew on his own experience in the canticle it took him a lifetime to finish. That lover of nature's beauty first called on all creation to join him in praise of the Creator: Brother Sun and Sister Moon, Wind, Air and Fire, Sister Earth:

All praise be yours, my Lord, through all
    that you have made.
    And first my lord Brother Sun,
    Who brings the day; and light you give to
    us through him.
How beautiful he is, how radiant in all his
    splendor!
    Of you, Most High, he bears the likeness.
All praise be yours, my Lord, through Sister
    Moon and Stars;
    In the heavens you have made them,
    bright
    And precious and fair.

A successful attempt to mediate peace in a bitter quarrel between the civil and religious authorities of Assisi inspired another verse:

All praise be yours, my Lord, through those
    who grant pardon
    For love of you; through those who
    endure
    Sickness and trial.
Happy those who endure in peace,
    By you, Most High, they will be crowned.

And when his life was drawing to a close, he added a final stanza:

15

All praise be yours, my Lord, through
   Sister Death,
      From whose embrace no mortal can
         escape.

Your song of praise, like that of Francis, is still a
lifetime away from completion. Over the span of a
long life together, you will add to it verses spun of joy
and tragedy: the miracle of giving birth, the joys and
worries of raising a family or the ache of infertility, the
anxiety of your middle years and the peace of old age,
the pain of final parting and the sure hope of reunion.
   Begin it now. Take pencil and paper and
separately write your own canticles. They needn't be
lengthy and they certainly don't have to be perfect
poetry. They need only reflect the wonder in your own
hearts. Weave into them the names you chose
yesterday to describe God. Give your reasons for
praise, the evidence you have seen of divine activity in
your lives and in your world. Look to the prayers of
the wedding liturgy for inspiration, if you like. This
Preface, for example, sings of human love:

   You created [us] in love to share your
      divine life.
   We see [our] high destiny in the love of
      husband and wife,
   which bears the imprint of your own
      divine love.
   Love is [our] origin,
   love is [our] constant calling,
   love is [our] fulfillment in heaven.
                              (*Rite of Marriage*)

Your prayer might speak of the gift God has given you in each other, of loneliness and isolation banished, of a new sense of your own value, of the life-giving power of love—whatever intimations of God your love has revealed to you.

Invite others to join in your song of praise, if you wish: your lover, all lovers, the angels and saints, the community of believers with whom you identify. Or imitate Francis and join your voice with the voices of all creation: Brother Sun and Sister Moon, the silent music of space, the songs of birds in the air and whales in the ocean.

When you have written your canticles, come together to pray them. Settle together into silence, into the presence of God. Read your canticles aloud, slowly and quietly, letting each of your hearts enter into the other's prayer.

Keep your songs of praise and come back to them often. Try to form them into one prayer you can pray together. Add to it as the years of your marriage roll by.

Day Four

Giving Thanks

Once you were strangers. Then you met, and your story began to unfold. Its beginning is unique to each couple: "I kissed her on the playground when we were in the second grade." "The day I met him I called my mother and told her I'd found the man I was going to marry." "We knew each other for years before we began to date." "It was just a summer romance, but when fall came I couldn't bear the thought of leaving town." Suddenly or slowly, early in life or late, you fell in love.

By now you have banked many precious memories. Some you will hand down to your children and grandchildren; others are private moments only the two of you will ever share. All of them are reasons for giving thanks to the God whose will is your love and happiness.

God's will doesn't always have such a good reputation. When sickness or sorrow strikes, believers use the phrase in an attempt to find meaning in pain. "It's God's will," they say. "There is a reason. Some good must surely come of it."

The risk in that attitude is forgetting that life's joys are no less God's will. We were made for happiness—everlasting happiness—according to the old *Baltimore Catechism*. One spiritual writer carries that idea a step

further and insists that we were made for ecstasy. And
so we were. God's will is traced up and down the
pages of our lives in small gifts and great: in the taste
of ice cream on a hot summer day, an autumn walk in
the woods, a bubble of laughter rising in our throats, in
the discovery of love and the yearning to share a
lifetime. To believe in God's will is to nurture a
grateful heart which remembers God's good gifts.

The followers of Jesus do just that regularly. At his
last meal with his friends, Jesus thanked the God he
called Father as his ancestors had done for centuries:
over the ordinary gifts of bread and wine. He added
new wording to the ancient prayers and spoke of his
body, which was about to be broken on the cross, and
of the blood he was to shed for the life of the world.
And he asked his disciples to repeat the gesture and
remember him as they did so.

When his people gather for the Lord's Supper,
they give thanks to the Father of Jesus for God's many
gifts, especially the gift of Jesus' life, death and
resurrection. The Eucharistic (the very word means
"thanksgiving") Prayer begins with an invitation to
nurture a grateful heart: "Let us give thanks to the
Lord our God." And then the story is retold:

> Through all eternity you live in
>   unapproachable light.
> Source of life and goodness, you have
>   created all things
> to fill your creatures with every blessing
> and lead all...to the joyful vision of your
>   light....
>
> Father, you so loved the world
> that in the fullness of time you sent your
>   only Son to be our Savior....

To the poor he proclaimed the good news of
    salvation,
to prisoners freedom,
and to those in sorrow, joy.
In fulfillment of your will
he gave himself up to death;
but by rising from the dead,
he destroyed death and restored life.
                                    (Eucharistic Prayer IV)

In today's prayer, borrow the pattern of the eucharistic
liturgy. Set out a simple snack to share—a crusty roll
and a glass of wine, cheese and crackers and your
favorite soft drink or whatever a search of the
refrigerator yields. Make yourselves comfortable and
relax in the silence where God moves for a few
minutes. Then begin to tell each other your story and
thank God for having written so much between the
lines.

Begin before history. Imagine the planet cooling
and life beginning to evolve until at last there are
human creatures, capable of tenderness and fidelity,
and thank God for the gift of human life.

Recall what you know of your family history, of
the forces and events which brought your ancestors
together, of how your parents met and married and
gave birth to you. Thank God for the gifts your
families gave you: for love and nurture, for the spiral
of DNA which is your genetic heritage and the
unrepeated pattern for the unique person each of you
is. Speak to each other of your best childhood
memories, of the movements that brought you
together in the place where you met.

Retell the story of your love: first impressions,
wonderful discoveries about each other, special

moments you shared, when and how you decided to marry. Thank God for bringing you together.

Thank God for the people who support you in your love for one another, the friends and family members whose names you put on the wedding invitation list. Give thanks for the people who have shaped your faith and influenced your decision to marry in church. Recall your good experiences of liturgy, the times when you, like the disciples who met Jesus on the road to Emmaus (see Luke 24:13-35), recognized the Lord in the breaking of the bread.

In the company of the Giver of all good gifts, offer each other the food you have prepared. Enjoy it.

Blessing Your Surroundings

You chose your wedding rings with great care, for they are the only pieces of jewelry you will wear day in and day out for the rest of your lives. New, they are bright with promise. Over the years they will thin and their polished surface will soften, but they will still speak the promise of enduring love you give each other in marriage. At your wedding, you name your rings what they are: a sign of love and fidelity. Shakespeare's young Richard III has prettier words for the ring he gives his love, but their meaning is the same:

> Look how this ring encompasseth thy finger,
> Even so thy breast encloses my poor heart;
> Wear both of them, for both of them are thine.

A prayer of blessing precedes the exchange of rings at a wedding. It asks God to help you make the sign ring true:

> May these rings be a symbol
> of true faith in each other,

and always remind them of their love.
(*Rite of Marriage*)

Prayers of blessing are as old as belief. They are closely bound to the prayers of praise and thanksgiving you explored on the previous two days of your novena. They reflect the conviction that God's love can be traced in the created world; they acknowledge the gifts already given and ask for God's continuing care.

Today's prayer is a series of blessings: for the house or apartment which is the first home of your marriage, for your bed and your table, those twin centers of daily married life, and for each other. It offers words for your use, but feel free to use your own words or to add to these. Take turns reading the paragraphs of each prayer; that will give you each an easy opportunity to add your own words.

Use holy water if you like (blessed itself as a reminder of its life-giving powers in nature and in Baptism); you can fill a small bottle in your parish church. Or carry a lighted candle, or simply extend your hands in the classic gesture of blessing.

Begin at your front door (inside, if attracting neighbors' stares makes you uneasy). Sprinkle it with holy water or hold out your hands and pray:

> Bless this door which opens into our home.
> May it always mark for us a refuge from
>   loneliness and anxiety.
> May we go from it full of strength to face the
>   challenges of the day.
> May we return to it eager for each other's
>   company.
>
> Bless this door which opens to our guests.
> May it welcome the friends and families who

support our life together.
May our hospitality be warm and gracious.

Bless this door which divides our home from
   the rest of the world.
May we never hide behind it from others'
   needs.
May we open it and our hearts to all who cry
   out for our compassion.

Add your own wishes. Then turn away from the door
toward the interior of your home. Sprinkle it with holy
water or extend your hands and pray:

Bless this home where our marriage begins.
Fill it with love and laughter.
Grace it with forgiveness when that is our
   need.

Bless this home for which we will care.
Make us thoughtful in our daily tasks and
   patient with each other.
May we sweep it free of dissension and
   anger.

Bless this home where we will live together.
Keep us close and faithful in love.
Dwell with us in this home and in our hearts.

Add your own wishes. Then go to your table, sprinkle
it with holy water or extend your hands over it and
pray:

Bless this table where we will share our
   meals.
Bless it with hope in the morning and joy in
   the evening.

Keep it filled with good things to eat.
May the food we consume here strengthen
us for a long and healthy life together.

Bless this table where people we love
will gather.
Give us faithful friends and loving families.
Keep us mindful of those who have neither
food nor love to share.
Nurture in us generosity which reflects
your own.

Bless this table which we hope to surround
with a family of our own.
Let it hear the sound of laughter.
Make us wise and loving parents, our
children healthy.
Be ever part of our family, our constant
guest.

Add your own wishes. Then go to your bedroom.
Sprinkle your bed with holy water or extend your
hands over it and pray:

Bless this bed which we will share.
May we find here rest from every care in
each other's arms.
May our sleep be untroubled by anxiety and
filled with bright dreams.

Bless this bed where we will make love.
May we give great pleasure and find great
wonder in each other.
May the union of our bodies express and
nourish the union of our hearts.

Bless this bed where we hope in season to
   conceive children.
Let us share your power to give life.
Touch our hearts with wonder at the
   miracles you accomplish in us.

Bless this bed where we will lie in illness.
Give us healing and courage when sickness
   comes.
Make the comfort we offer each other tender
   and caring.

Add your own wishes, then turn toward each other.
Trace a cross on each other's forehead with holy water
or lay your hands on each other's head and pray in
turn:

May the God who has given you to me
   bless you always.
May God keep your love for me strong
   and true.
May you find me always a joy, God's
   greatest blessing to you.
May God keep you well and give us a long
   life together.

Close with the blessing Jacob spoke many centuries
ago:

The LORD watch between you and me,
when we are absent one from the other.
                                    (Genesis 31:49)

Day Six

Exploring Scripture

Planning the first Easter dinner in her new home, a bride asked her mother how to cook a leg of lamb. "Be sure to have the butcher cut the shank off," Mom advised. "Why?" asked the bride. "I don't know," her mother replied. "That's what *my* mother always did."

Curious, the bride called her grandmother for an explanation. "Because I didn't have a pan big enough to hold the whole leg," Grandma laughed. Thus are family traditions born.

And when the bride reported the story to her new husband, his reaction surprised her. "Lamb? Ham is what you have for Easter dinner!" Such is the power of tradition.

Each of you brings to your marriage a rich history of family and ethnic traditions. They range from the trivial—which way to roll the toilet paper in the bathroom or hang the icicles on the Christmas tree—to the essential—proper roles for husband and wife. Some of them simply no longer work in our changing world. (Few women of your generation will adopt the life-styles of their mothers and grandmothers without major alterations, for example.) Many of them will find their way into the heritage you pass on to future generations. Over the years you will sort through your combined heritages, discarding some things, blending others and adding new ideas until you have created a blend of traditions which is uniquely yours.

The family of believers has a rich heritage of traditions, too. Every now and then the whole family has to sort through the treasure chest, see what no longer works and add some new ideas. The Second Vatican Council was just such a sorting-out process. In its wake, out went mandatory Friday abstinence, in came liturgy in your native tongue. More importantly, every new generation must sort through the heritage as adult individuals, making the essentials truly their own and incorporating whatever else seems relevant into their religious life.

Choosing the readings for your wedding is part of that process. From the wealth of Scripture, the Church asks you to choose for your wedding liturgy a few passages that reflect your personal faith and your vision of marriage. Today's prayer invites you to reflect more deeply on one of the readings you have chosen or are considering and to pray together over it. You will need a Bible, preferably a modern translation with good notes and cross-references. (*The New American Bible* and *The New Jerusalem Bible* are excellent.)

The Bible reaches much further back into tradition than most families. Countless generations recorded in its pages their experience of God's activity in their world. And many more generations have recognized in their ancestors' reflections so much undying truth that they call this book inspired by God. But its truths are often clothed in terms which no longer seem to hold meaning. Evolutionists and creationists quarrel over the accuracy of the creation account, yet the truth Genesis embodies stands: However we came into being, we are God's handiwork, made male and female as images of God's creative love.

A book (more accurately, a collection of books) written by many people in many eras doesn't lend itself to quick, uncritical reading. Each passage rests in a particular historical and cultural context. Yet there is an overarching theme—God reaches out to us in love—which is played and replayed with countless variations. However appealing or jarring one passage may be at first reading, its message cannot be fully grasped without seeing it in relation to the rest of the Bible.

So before you begin your prayer, do a little homework together. Pick one of the wedding readings and find it in the Bible. (The table of contents will help you find the book; use the chapter and verse numbers to locate the passage. To find 1 Cor 12:31—13:8, for example, turn to Paul's First Letter to the Corinthians, chapter 12, verse 31, and read through the eighth verse of chapter 13.)

Read the introduction to the book to find out when, where and under what circumstances it was written. Check the footnotes for further information on the historical context. Try to imagine what life was like in that time and place.

Then try to think of other passages you have read or heard which shed further light on this passage. You don't have to name chapter and verse; just try to recall coming across Scripture with a similar message or picking up a few historical facts that help you make better sense of this passage. If your Bible offers cross-references to this reading, look up those passages and read them.

Finally, take a close look at your reading. Who is speaking or acting? Who is listening or observing? Read as much of the surrounding text as you need for a good sense of what is happening.

Now you are ready to begin your prayer. In the 16th century, St. Ignatius of Loyola developed a set of spiritual exercises still popular today. At their heart lies a method of using your imagination to put yourself into a scriptural passage, to hear and see and get emotionally involved.

Settle again into quiet. Then create with your own words the scene where these words are first spoken. Describe the physical surroundings: the lush Garden of Eden, the room filled with the first Christians waiting to hear someone read a letter from an apostle, the afternoon sun warming a dusty hillside in Galilee. Recreate the mood of the people who are there.

Read your passage aloud, taking turns being speaker/doer and listener/observer or the different characters involved. Then switch roles and read it again.

Be quiet for a moment and let your imaginations have their way. Then express your reactions to each other. With whom did you identify most strongly? What did you think or feel as you listened? How do these words relate to your concept of Church, your religious upbringing?

Finally, address God in your own words. Tell the Lord what hopes and fears, experiences and dreams this reading touched. Give thanks and praise in your own way.

Day Seven

Finding the Way

Many, many years ago, two young people agreed
to marry. But then something awful happened:
The young man found out his bride-to-be was
pregnant, and he knew the baby wasn't his.

According to the laws of their society, they had
entered into an agreement as binding as marriage.
Should he announce what he knew, the woman would
be found guilty of adultery—a crime that demanded
the death penalty. Hurt as he was, the young man
couldn't bring himself to expose the woman he loved
to such a fate. He did a lot of thinking. Surely he
prayed, for he was a man of faith. Finally he decided a
quiet divorce would be a better solution.

That night, as he tossed and turned in his bed, he
had a dream. An angelic voice spoke to him: "Joseph,
son of David, do not be afraid to take Mary as your
wife, for the child conceived in her is from the Holy
Spirit. She will bear a son, and you are to name him
Jesus, for he will save his people from their sins"
(Matthew 1:20b-21). And you know the rest of the
story.

Most of us don't get such clear directions. Angels
appear in precious few bedrooms and even the most
vivid dreams are unlikely to leave a clear impression
of what we should do in the morning. A handful of

people speak of a clear call or a sudden flash of insight into their life's intended direction. But God doesn't show most of us the blueprint our lives are supposed to follow—if indeed God has such a blueprint tucked away in heaven's vault. Mostly we make decisions— even major decisions—without explicit divine guidance.

Or do we? Perhaps those who get clear direction merely know how to listen more keenly. Joseph, after all, had to trust in his dream. He had listened to his heart and decided not to expose Mary to judgment. He had reasoned well and carefully toward his decision not to take Mary as his wife. He could have blamed the dream on eating too many ripe figs before he went to bed or reaching too many times for the goatskin of wine in an effort to take the edge off his pain. But the angel's voice echoed what his heart and mind already knew of Mary.

Many choices lie ahead of you in your life together. Sometimes you will wish an angel would appear and tell you what to do. Today's prayer is an exercise in trust—the kind of trust that will sharpen your listening skills when you face important choices in the years ahead.

You have already made probably the most momentous decision of your lives: to marry. That decision sprang from your hearts, of course, from the love which has taken root there. You made it with your bodies, too, out of the wonderful chemistry which attracts you to each other physically. And you made it with your minds as you considered all the practical ramifications of your choice. In other words, you decided with your whole selves to give your whole selves to one another for a lifetime.

And from the beginning, you invited input from

others. You introduced each other to family and friends and sought smiles of approval; you confided your deepening feelings to the people nearest to you. In the last months before your wedding, you met with your parish priest, perhaps with a married couple or with other engaged couples in some kind of marriage preparation program.

Perhaps you prayed over your decision. But whether you knew it or not, you conferred with God. For God speaks in many ways other than angelic visitations. God whispers in your very being, in the yearnings of your flesh, in the workings of your mind and in the movement of your heart. God speaks in the loving people who surround you and in the community of believers to which you belong.

The Psalms affirm that God's voice is heard in many ways. Those ancient prayers from Israel are both the most urgent individual prayers and songs the community of believers sang together. They express many moods. Some are songs of joy and thanksgiving; others sing the blues. Some cry out to a silent God; others beg forgiveness. Underlying all of them is one deep-down conviction: God cares for us and guides us with a loving hand.

That conviction is, for believers, the basis of all decision-making. Let the Psalms nurture your belief that God is near, speaking softly in your hearts and in the voices of others, and you will be better able to listen as you walk together through the future.

Pray the psalm below together. You can pray it in the same way people pray psalms after the first reading at Mass: One of you can read the verses and the other respond, perhaps with "Lord, we are in your hands." Or take turns reading the verses. Either way, the important thing is to hear the words with your

whole being and try to make their author's trust in
God's loving presence your own.

Relax into the silence of God's nearness for a few
minutes, and then begin.

O LORD, you have searched me and known me.
You know when I sit down and when I rise up;
    you discern my thoughts from far away.
You search out my path and my lying down,
    and are acquainted with all my ways.

Even before a word is on my tongue,
    O LORD, you know it completely.
You hem me in, behind and before,
    and lay your hand upon me.
Such knowledge is too wonderful for me;
    it is so high I cannot attain it.

Where can I go from your spirit?
    Or where can I flee from your presence?
If I ascend to heaven, you are there;
    if I make my bed in She'ol, you are there.
If I take the wings of the morning
    and settle at the farthest limits of the sea,
even there your hand shall lead me,
    and your right hand shall hold me fast.

If I say, "Surely the darkness shall cover me,
    and the light around me become night,"
even the darkness is not dark to you;
    the night is as bright as the day,
    for darkness is as light to you.

For it was you who formed my inward parts;
    you knit me together in my mother's womb.
I praise you, for I am fearfully and
    wonderfully made.

Wonderful are your works;
that I know very well.

My frame was not hidden from you,
when I was being made in secret,
  intricately woven in the depths of the earth.

Your eyes beheld my unformed substance.
In your book were written
  all the days that were formed for me,
when none of them yet existed.

(Psalm 139:1-16)

Tell each other how you came to know you wanted to spend your lives together. How did God guide you toward your decision?

Seeking Forgiveness

Many centuries ago a Greek philosopher spun a tale of humanity's beginnings. At first, he said, there was but one kind of human. Then the gods, angered at some impertinence, split the creatures in two, forming men and women. From that day on, each person must seek the lost half and, on finding it, cling to it forever.

Genesis, too, speaks of regained wholeness: Adam embraces the woman whose frame is his own rib. Both stories contain a truth lovers know: Falling in love is like finding the other half of yourself, the half you never before knew was missing.

The differences between you are as precious as the interests and values you share. Your personalities make a new whole as surely as your bodies are designed to do: talkative *and* quiet, practical *and* imaginative, impulsive *and* cautious, feminine *and* masculine.

Unfortunately, as you have no doubt already discovered, those differences can also prove irritating. You do not always understand each other, no matter how hard you try. And misunderstanding breeds anger and erupts into quarrels. You hurt each other—sometimes without meaning to, sometimes without realizing why your actions are painful. Furthermore, in opening your hearts to each other, you have given each other great power to inflict wounds. When one of you feels mean, he or she knows exactly where to put the knife.

And hurt each other you will—many times in the course of your life together. Whether the issues are minor—who does which household chores or whether or not civilized people carry on conversations first thing in the morning—or such serious rifts as a major clash in values or a lapse from fidelity, your marriage will keep the savor of love only if you season it with generous portions of forgiveness.

Today's prayer is an exercise in bringing your need to forgive and be forgiven to the expert: the God Scripture constantly describes as merciful and compassionate.

Before you begin, consider what it means to forgive. The word literally means "to give before"—to extend to each other acceptance of your differences, to be willing to take delight in each other even when understanding fails.

It's not quite that simple, though. The gift is first given before you ever injure each other, but you must give it over and over again as scars multiply. Forgiveness after the fact is an expression of trust restored, of a new willingness to accept someone with a proven ability to inflict hurt.

The God Jesus called Father extends that kind of acceptance to each of us. Like a loving parent, God delights in your uniqueness, in the curious blend of strength and weakness each of us is. For the truth is that virtue and fault are difficult to separate. Even how we name them depends on circumstances. The carefree spontaneity that enriches one of you on one day becomes the impulsiveness that annoys you on another; the perseverance that will help carry both of you through a rough time is also the stubbornness against which one of you rails.

What you *are* will probably not change much over your lifetime. Thank God for that—what you are is what you love in each other. What you *do* is another matter. What you do always flows from what you are, from the way you respond to events, but what you do can be hurtful.

To recover your joy in each other usually takes three steps: bringing the hurt into the open, accepting responsibility and rediscovering your reasons for loving each other. There are many ways to take those steps. This eighth day of your novena invites you to pray your way to reconciliation.

Relax your minds and bodies and settle into silence. Reflect for a few minutes on the trait in your lover which most baffles and annoys you.

Aloud, in your own words, confess to the God who knit each of you in your mother's womb what that trait is and what effect it has on you. Admit your difficulty in dealing with it. Don't make accusations, just express your own feelings. Tell God how different the two of you are. Ask God to help you understand the way the other ticks.

Such a conversation might sound like this:

> You know I love Joe. But I have a hard time finding out what he's thinking. When we have a decision to make together, I want to talk about the pros and cons and come to a conclusion right now. He just sits there or

says he'll think about it. I feel shut out.
Please help me understand what's going on
in his mind. Help me be patient with his
style—it's so different from my own.

Be still in God's presence for a few minutes and listen
to what you have heard. Acknowledge the reality of
who you are. Then admit to God the truth your lover
has spoken. Like this:

You know I love Alyssa. But sometimes I get
paralyzed when she wants me to move
faster. It's hard for me to think out loud. It
takes time for me to figure out what I think
or feel. So I retreat from her. I can see her
frustration, but I don't know how to
respond. Help me to make it better, to find
the space I need without hurting her.

Return to the silence and consider how the differences
you have aired complement each other. What strength
do you draw from them? How do they complete you?
    Then confide those findings to God in each other's
hearing. Name other ways your lover makes you feel
whole, and thank God for giving you to each other.
    To close your prayer, pray together the Our
Father, the prayer Jesus taught. Say it slowly,
remembering that the God who formed you loves each
of you just as you are. Exchange a kiss of peace as a
pledge of your willingness to do the same.

Day Nine

Presenting Needs

There are, the saying goes, no atheists in foxholes. When life hangs in the balance, even unbelievers cry out for help. Indeed, it was a foxhole prayer that startled John Newton into penning the words that became the popular hymn "Amazing Grace" (see page 6).

To believers, crying out to God from any need comes quite naturally. The habit is rooted in confidence that God cares what happens to us, in faith in divine love. That kind of prayer is surely so familiar to you it hardly seems to need a place in this novena. An exercise in petitionary prayer hardly seems necessary. No wonder it is last in this novena.

But is it really so easy to expose your need to God in each other's presence? Showing need is, in common thought, a sign of weakness, even vulnerability. It's all very well to let God see your needy side; it's much harder to show it to another human being.

"I need you": That's what you in some way managed to say to each other in the season of courtship. It was a risky statement. Either of you could have refused the need, inflicting the terrible pain of rejection. Yet somehow each of you sensed that the other already knew, already wanted to fill your hunger. The measure of your love is the willingness you have shown to speak your need to each other.

The measure of your love for God is not so different. Believers speak their needs to God out of a sense that God already knows their hunger and already waits to satisfy it. Faith says that God hears the longings of your hearts before you can frame them in words. Faith says that God waits with infinite patience for you to speak your needs.

The Church's certainty that you will want to speak your needs to God is the reason why planning your wedding liturgy includes naming the needs to be mentioned in the Prayer of the Faithful. Like most brides and grooms, you probably thought first of your wishes for your own enduring love, of your gratitude for the people who support you and of the painful absence of those who cannot attend your wedding because they are distanced from you by miles or death.

But the Prayer of the Faithful ranges farther than your personal yearnings. It is literally the prayer of the *faith-filled*—the people who believe that God listens to anyone who prays in the name of the beloved Son. In the liturgy it serves as a bridge between the Liturgy of the Word and the Liturgy of the Eucharist—between the part of the Mass in which the searching can participate and the meal which rightfully belongs only to the family gathered by Jesus. In the infant Church people who were exploring the new way of Jesus were gently dismissed before the baptized offered their petitions. In today's Church, catechumens again leave the building after the homily, and the baptized then lift their voices in prayer.

That doesn't mean God refuses prayer from anyone. God doesn't check churchgoing credentials; God's heart beats in rhythm with any human need. But the prayer of believers differs from foxhole prayer in one important way: It reaches beyond personal need. The Church even directs the Prayer of the Faithful— the prayer of believers—in specific directions. It includes four categories of need: the needs of the Church, of the world and its authorities, of those oppressed by any kind of pain and of the local community.

The liturgical guidelines reflect the reality of human love. Love refuses containment. Lovers feel benevolent toward the whole world. Lovers are sensitive to any pain and need they sense, for love gives a clear vision of God's will for the world.

"Thy kingdom come, thy will be done," you prayed on the eighth day of this novena. In God's kingdom, there is no sorrow, no loss, no enmity or estrangement. In God's kingdom there is only joy, only sure confidence in God's care. God's will for all humanity is the wholeness you have found in loving each other.

Pray, then, in solidarity with all who hunger for the love you have found, using the designated categories of the Prayer of the Faithful as a guide. Observe just one caution: Leave the answers in God's hands. That may sound obvious, but human nature always wants to wrest control. In prayer, that effort turns praying *for* into praying *that*, demanding solutions of the Lord. You have surely heard prayers phrased that way in your parish, but it's not a good model of Christian prayer.

Settle into the silence you know so well. Listen to your hearts, to the wisdom your love has implanted there. And then speak your petitions as they occur to you. Answer each other as you do in church: "Lord, hear our prayer."

Pray for the needs of the Church. Pray out of your

own experience of Church, out of what you read in the newspapers and hear from the pulpit—for faith, understanding, wise leadership; for the courage to speak out, the wisdom with which to touch an unbelieving world, the grace to respect other beliefs.

Pray for the needs of the world and its leaders. Pray from the headlines: for peace, for patience, for justice, for compassion, for the planet itself.

Pray for the human needs you see: for the hungry, the homeless, the sorrowing, the lonely, the sick, the oppressed and the persecuted. Draw on your own experience and the experience of people you have loved.

Pray for the local community, your own small world: the family and friends who have taught you love, the people who have helped you prepare for marriage, the parish which has nurtured or disappointed you. Pray for yourselves: for ever-deepening faith and love.

Another Day

Beginning Again

You have tested the waters of shared prayer and, I hope, found them refreshing. Where do you go from here?

Back to the beginning. You can make your way through the nine days again. Your life together will work enough changes in your faith and your needs to make this novena a new experience.

Make some changes in each day's prayer, if you like. Here are a few suggestions for starters (don't hesitate to add your own):

Day One: Listen to the silence against a different background. Go outside. Find a spot where nature sings: a park, the woods, the beach, a riverbank. Listen to birds singing, rain or snow falling, a gentle breeze or an approaching thunderstorm. Move to a different place inside: the kitchen, the fireside, your bedroom. Play some meditative music and listen to the silence it leaves behind.

Day Two: Reflect on the image of God you had when you were a child, a teenager. Try to capture someone else's image of God: your parents' or grandparents', your friends', some public figure's. Explore the likenesses and the differences between those images and your own. Search Scripture—your wedding readings or the Sunday readings—and try to define the image of God presented there. Focus on the Trinity: Father, Son and Spirit. What is your image of each Person?

Day Three: Look for "The Canticle of Brother Sun" by St. Francis in your parish or civic library. Write a paraphrase, substituting the work of human hands for the beauties of nature. Find out who sings these biblical songs of praise and pray with them: Exodus 15:1-18; 1 Samuel 2:1-10; Psalms 147, 149 and 150; Luke 1:68-79. Sing together a song of praise you sing at liturgy.

Day Four: Pray each of the Eucharistic Prayers (you can find them in a parish missalette) and decide which one best expresses your thanks at liturgy. Recall the sorrows you have experienced and give thanks for what you learned or overcame. Search the headlines for reasons to give thanks. Give thanks for the people who have enriched your life in some way—and decide how to deliver your thanks to them. Discuss how you can express your gratitude by giving of your time or money to someone less fortunate.

Day Five: Bless your lover by tracing a cross on each other's forehead when you part for the day's activities and come together at day's end. Experiment with different table graces to bless the meals you share. Bless each other's bodies, head to toe. Bless the things which make your home a pleasant place: the furnace, the faucets, the windows, your record collection, your favorite chairs. Bless the car that carries you safely away from home and back again.

Day Six: Use the same technique to explore another of your wedding readings, a passage from the Sunday liturgy or your favorite Scripture passage. Read parallel passages in the Gospels and compare them. (Try the Sermon on the Mount: Matthew 5—7 and Luke 6:20-49; the miracle of the loaves and fishes: Matthew 14:13-21, Mark 6:30-44, Luke 9:10-17 and John 6:1-14; the Last Supper: Matthew 26:26-29, Mark 14:22-25 and Luke 22:15-20; the Resurrection: Matthew 28:1-10, Mark 16:1-11, Luke 24:1-12 and John 20:1-18.)

Day Seven: Talk about other decisions you have made and how they affected your lives. How did you come to the decision? How did God guide you then? Sing or play a recording of Dan Schutte, S.J.'s, musical version of Psalm 139, "You Are Near." Pray these other Psalms which express trust: 11, 23, 27, 62, 121 and 131.

Day Eight: Pray about what you consider your own deepest flaws, and let your lover plead your case to God. Pray your way through the first quarrel you had or a time when one of you hurt the other and found forgiveness. Pray over injuries from others you have had trouble forgiving and try to see God's view of the person who hurt you. And, of course, pray over anything which stands between you at the moment.

Day Nine: Address your intercessions to Mary and ask her to present them to her Son for you.

Another way to alter this novena is to direct it to Mary or to some other favorite saint. If a particular day's prayer strains your imaginations beyond their limits, skip over it. Here is a brief overview of a novena to Mary:

Day One: Listen in the silence for the powerful God of Israel, the God who saves a people from oppression, and for the presence of Israel's faithful daughter, your mother.

Day Two: Pray the Marian litany, the Litany of Loretto. Or pray to her under whatever titles appeal to you.

Day Three: Pray the Magnificat (Luke 1:46-55).

Day Four: Mary is both loving mother and model disciple. Thank her for her example and for her intercession on your behalf.

Day Five: Invite Mary into your home, beginning at the front door. Ask her to imbue it with her goodness.

Day Six: Explore a passage in which Mary appears: Luke 1:26-38 (the Annunciation); Luke 1:39-45 (the Visitation); Luke 2:22-38 (the Presentation); Luke 2:41-52 (finding Jesus in the temple); John 2:1-12 (the miracle at Cana); John 19:25-27 (Mary at Calvary); Acts 1:13-14 (waiting for the Spirit's coming).

Day Seven: Picture Mary agreeing to bear Jesus or holding her son's dead body in her arms. How did she express her trust in God?

Day Eight: Imagine a meeting between Mary and Judas after Good Friday. Or run to Mary's lap for comfort in all your failures.

Day Nine: Present your concerns to Mary, the mother who intercedes for us all.

Here's an even briefer overview of the novena addressed to St. Francis of Assisi to show how you can adapt it to your favorite saint:

Day One: Seek the God of creation.

Day Two: Name God Creator. How does that God invite you to participate in the work of creation?

Day Three: Pray Francis' Canticle.

Day Four: Give thanks for the gifts of creation.

Day Five: Bless the wonders in your backyard.

Day Six: Explore the passage that seized Francis' heart—Luke 10:1-9.

Day Seven: Reflect on what Francis learned from defeat in war, illness and poverty.

Day Eight: Pray or sing the Prayer of St. Francis.

Day Nine: Pray with Francis for the needs of the poor; embrace the "leper" in your life as he did.

However you pray together, make it a lifelong habit!

Other Prayer Resources From St. Anthony Messenger Press

The Blessing Cup: 24 Simple Rites for Family Prayer-Celebrations, by Rock Travnikar, O.F.M. (B8601, $2.95)

Breaking Open the Gospel of Luke, by Gerard P. Weber and Robert Miller (B1388, $5.95)

The Forgiving Family: First Steps to Reconciliation, by Carol Luebering (B0276, $2.50)

His Word: Letting It Take Root—and Bear Fruit—in Our Lives, by David Knight (B0489, $3.95)

Journeys Into Mark: 16 Lessons of Exploration and Discovery, by Raymond Apicella (B1124, $4.95)

Marriage: Sacrament of Hope and Challenge, by William P. Roberts (B1027, $6.95)

101 Meal Prayers for Christians, compiled by Theresa Cotter (I1011, $9.95)

Sharing Prayer: Simple Formats for Small Groups, by Mary Sue Taylor (B0861, $5.95)

Available from
St. Anthony Messenger Press
1615 Republic St.
Cincinnati, OH 45210
513-241-5615